Praise for *Enterprise Agreements – Made Easy*

This book actually achieves what the title suggests by providing the reader with simple to understand guidance on the process of negotiating enterprise agreements under the Australian industrial relations framework. From researching, preparing and planning to the final agreement, this text has everything that a HR practitioner needs to confidently embark on the journey of enterprise bargaining.

The authors have cleverly used their practical knowledge and experience to provide a suite of case studies and checklists to ensure that all contingencies that may arise are covered from an employer perspective. The practical need to identify what is sought to be achieved with an enterprise agreement and the attendant risks of entering into a negotiating phase are all suitably dealt with in a forthright and concise manner. With the essential technical knowledge provided and while leaving nothing to chance, the book is free from legal rhetoric and extensive references to case law and statutes, enabling the reader to concentrate on the principles of enterprise bargaining.

For the HR practitioner or operational manager all aspects of dealing with employees, unions and senior management are covered, including what is commonly overlooked in securing the support and commitment of the senior executive team before commencing the task of securing or replacing an enterprise agreement with employees.

This text is an essential and contemporary reference book for any novice negotiator and a handy reference tool for the more seasoned practitioner and will indeed make the task of enterprise agreement making an easier exercise!

~ Deputy President Geoff Bull, Fair Work Commission.

If only all enterprise agreements were as easy to read as this book! Tammy and Rachael have done an excellent job in translating their extensive experience into this practical "how to guide" for employers.

While the book does not over simplify the enterprise bargaining process (which for many employers is a significant event in terms of time, resources and risk), it certainly presents sensible suggestions in a straightforward way with well-organised chapters containing excellent summaries, handy hints, case studies and checklists to reinforce the recommendations provided.

This book not only encourages those involved in the enterprise agreement process to be prepared but, provides useful step by step guidance on how to do that preparation. It is a must have resource for any employer representative about to start the enterprise agreement journey.

For first timers it provides a clear and simple road map to help prepare for the journey and to navigate along the way. For those who have been down this road before it will give them ideas on how to avoid some of the potholes they will no doubt have experienced in the past.

I will be recommending "Enterprise Agreements - Made Easy" to my clients as a must have reference point to assist with a quicker and smoother enterprise agreement journey.

~ Kylie Groves, Partner, Squire Patton Boggs

ENTERPRISE AGREEMENTS

MADE EASY

National Library of Australia Cataloguing-in-Publication data:

Creator: McGann, Rachael, author.

Title: Enteprise agreements - made easy / Rachael McGann, Tammy Tansley.

ISBN: 9780994305930 (paperback)

Notes: Includes index.

Subjects: Australia. Fair Work Act 2009. Wage bargaining--Australia. Collective labor agreements--Australia. Other Creators/Contributors:

Tansley, Tammy, author.

Dewey Number: 344.940189

Printed in the United States of America

Jacket Design: Kelly Exeter

Book Design: Kelly Exeter

First Edition

For my father James (Jim) McGann—International HR and IR Guru, who taught me that developing mutual respect provides much better outcomes than starting a fight. And for My Mother Carole, the strongest and smartest woman I know. Finally to Peter Taylor, my life is so much better with you in it. All my love, Rachael

For Alex and my mischiefs—with love and thanks again. And to Maxine and Marcia, who gave me the best possible grounding in Industrial Relations – thank you. Tammy

ABOUT THE AUTHORS

RACHAEL MCGANN

Rachael is an HR and IR professional with over 25 years' experience in national and multinational organisations in Australia and around the globe. Rachael has held senior executive roles with HR and IR responsibility for Asia-Pacific, Europe, the Middle East and Africa. With extensive experience across a broad variety of industries in both the public and private sectors, since 2009 Rachael has operated her own successful consultancy business (gerlanconsulting.com) based in Melbourne.

Known as a very 'hands-on' HR practitioner with a pragmatic, creative but strategic approach to issues, Rachael is passionate about the contribution HR can make to the success of an organisation. She has a proven ability to drive change that supports business strategies, improves people performance and positively contributes to an improved bottom line.

A keen horse rider, Rachael lives 'on a few acres' with her partner Peter, four spoilt horses, two equally spoilt border collies, numerous cattle and countless resident kangaroos!

TAMMY TANSLEY

Tammy has negotiated agreements in almost every state in Australia. She has 25 years IR and HR experience in Australia and the United Kingdom. Tammy is the owner of Tammy Tansley Consulting (tammytansley.com.au). She has worked with leaders and organisations around the world on leadership, high performing teams, organisational culture and change; inspiring simple approaches to enable great people performance. She also co-owns Help Me HR (helpmehr.com.au).

This is Tammy's second book. Her first book *Do What You Say You'll Do* is a book for new leaders and those reinventing their leadership (dowhatyousay.com.au).

Tammy is married to Alex and lives in Perth with their two young daughters and two cats.

CONTENTS

ENTERPRISE AGREEMENTS

MADE EASY

Rachael McGann & Tammy Tansley

TAMMY TANSLEY CONSULTING
AUSTRALIA

INTRODUCTION

This is a short, practical book written for HR practitioners, operational managers and front line supervisors who are leading or participating in enterprise agreement negotiations in Australia.

The book is the culmination of many decades of experience negotiating enterprise agreements; we have learnt many lessons along the way and now we can share them with you and help to give you a bit of a head start! This book will help you read the industrial landscape at your workplace. It will help you understand the 'game' and be prepared to play it to negotiate the best deal for you and your organisation. Most of all, it will help remove some of the mystique from the process.

So, how can this book help you and your organisation? After all, there are plenty of great books around on learning how to negotiate. Often, we think about negotiation as the 'argy-bargy' of the face-to-face discussions, but a successful negotiation starts long before the parties first meet. This book is about the broader process of preparation, not just the meetings themselves. A good way to think about it is as a project and just like any other project; a negotiation needs planning, preparation and appropriate resources devoted to it.

What is Negotiation?

Negotiation typically is a process where two or more parties with different needs and goals discuss an issue to find a mutually acceptable solution. In enterprise bargaining terms this means that employer and employee representatives (union and/ or non-union) meet to negotiate an agreement that reflects employment terms and conditions, typically for the two or three years ahead. In some cases, this can mean simply a 'roll over' of the current terms with the exception of discussions around a wage increase, a pattern agreement (i.e. pattern bargaining occurs when a bargaining representative seeks to make identical agreements with two or more employers) or more commonly, it is a comprehensive negotiation addressing many or all of the terms and conditions in the agreement. This book focuses on the latter scenario.

Why is it Important?

Enterprise agreement negotiations are resource hungry and time consuming. They can have a huge impact on the organisation for years beyond the actual negotiation. Negotiating the best agreement possible will have an immediate impact and can help prepare an organisation, and its people, for success in the years to come.

Enterprise agreement negotiations are usually conducted with union officials who have much more experience and so there is often an imbalance. Being well prepared and having a good understanding of the process gives you the best possible chance to overcome this imbalance and deliver the best possible outcome for your organisation.

However, you may also find yourself bargaining directly with employees, in either a union or non-union negotiation, which can present its own challenges and complexities. This book is equally applicable in this circumstance and can support you and your employees through what can be a stressful process.

How do enterprise bargaining negotiations differ from other negotiations?

It's important to understand how enterprise bargaining negotiations are different to other negotiations (particularly commercial negotiations):

1. What makes the negotiation of agreements unique is that there are often political or industrial overtones that impact the 'enterprise' nature of the negotiations (see the case study below). These are often beyond the direct influence of any of the parties, especially the employer.

2. As you are often dealing with wages/hours/conditions that have a direct impact on employees' livelihoods, it's personal—the employee representatives aren't negotiating some random clause. Often the people who are negotiating will bear the outcomes (good and bad). This is different to a commercial negotiation, where the day-to-day impact and outcomes can be more removed from the people who are negotiating.

3. There are a significant number of legal requirements that underpin the process.

4. There is a perception that enterprise bargaining negotiations are/have to be adversarial and often people are not good at managing conflict.

5. Because of the nature of employee representatives, often the people you are negotiating with are then the ones that you need to work beside or manage in the workplace. They are also representing their colleagues, which can present other challenges.

Case Study

An organisation had been negotiating with a moderate union for a number of months around a charter of positive behaviour and engagement between the two parties. It was innovative and ground-breaking work and had reached a very promising point. There was then a state election. The incumbent party was ousted and to be replaced by a new Government. The whole tenor and tone of the negotiations changed. Ultimately, agreement wasn't reached.

Key Points to Consider:

- An enterprise agreement negotiation is a project and like any other project requires planning, preparation and adequate resources devoted to it.

- An enterprise agreement negotiation requires some specific skills and tactics that relate to the face-to-face meetings, but much of the work is done in the behind-the-scenes planning, research and communication.

- Negotiating the best agreement possible can have immediate implications but will also help set up an organisation for the future.

Checklist - Introduction

☑ Check out the key dates to start planning the negotiation project. Is there a current agreement? When is the nominal expiry date of that agreement? If it's a new agreement, are there any critical dates by which the agreement needs to be completed by?

☑ Access current information from the Fair Work Commission website. Start to read up on agreement requirements and any recent changes, particularly around the timely completion of paperwork.

☑ Look out for and if possible attend any seminars or information sessions on the industrial environment, IR legislation and industry trends.

☑ Start to develop your project plan. You can use the headings of the chapters of this book as a guide.

CHAPTER 1

Preparing the Organisation's Negotiation Team

It is probably a little obvious to say that the organisation's negotiation team can make or break the process, however, it is also fair to say that the importance of the team composition and preparation is often underestimated by organisations.

Staff employment costs are frequently 30% or more of the regular running cost of an organisation and an enterprise agreement may determine a significant proportion of that cost. Yet it is not unusual to see relatively junior HR staff, and/or staff with little or no industrial relations experience, made responsible for negotiating agreements that have significant cultural, operational and financial impacts.

In this chapter, we look at the steps an organisation can take to select, prepare and coordinate the negotiation team in order to maximise success and minimise risk.

Selecting the Organisation's Team

It is always useful if you have an indication of the number of employee representatives expected at the negotiation meeting. Typically the larger the organisation and scope of the agreement (e.g. covering a number of different locations, work classifications etc.), the greater the number of representatives you can expect. While you do not want to be hopelessly outnumbered, nor do you need to have a cast of thousands representing the organisation. However, you do need to ensure that you have both operational understanding of the relevant (impacted) work areas and sufficient understanding of industrial relations processes and requirements. So instead of thinking too much about team numbers, think carefully about the experience, knowledge and skill set that you require within that team.

Typically a team should be able to cover:

- Operational knowledge of the relevant work function/area(s).

- Operational knowledge of each location covered by the agreement (if multiple).

- Historical knowledge of previous agreement negotiations (not always easy to find, but can be very useful in meetings).

- Technical knowledge of the industrial relations legislation and regulation(s) and agreement requirements.

- Someone with the ability to appropriately draft clauses or make amendments to existing clauses.

- Financial/cost analysis and modelling skills.

- Negotiation experience, preferably with enterprise agreements.

- Someone with the authority to make decisions.

- Someone to take notes and minutes (sometimes considered a luxury, but invaluable for complex discussions—it is very hard to negotiate, listen properly, read the room and take notes at the same time).

Preparing the Organisation's Negotiating Team

With the above activities in mind, you should now assign these activities/roles to the team members to ensure you have all requirements covered. Most importantly a team leader needs to be identified, as this person (generally the most senior/experienced in the team) will act as the lead negotiator and spokesperson in meetings and in other key dealings with employee representatives.

It is most important that the organisation treats the negotiation as a priority. Ensure that managers provide the team members with time not only to attend the negotiation meetings but to actively participate in preparation and other associated team activities (meeting debriefs, strategy discussions, research etc.).

Negotiation training is also advised for those who have little or no experience in the area. Specific enterprise agreement negotiation training is something you do need to seek out, or find a provider who can tailor a more general course to the specifics you need. Usually, your local chamber of commerce and industry or industry association will be able to provide you some direction on this.

If at all possible, it is also a very good idea to provide all team members with some information and understanding of the enterprise agreement process and legal requirements (e.g. are there compulsory clauses, what is 'good faith bargaining'?). While negotiation training can help to provide structure and process, this training and information should provide context and highlight some of the specific IR, political and economic influences of an enterprise agreement negotiation. Even for more experienced team members such a session can still prove very useful, as the legislative environment changes constantly. Employer associations and specialist law firms often have great information sessions and updates on the enterprise agreement environment.

Negotiating Team Kick-off Meeting

This is an important meeting. It brings together everyone on your team, and lays out the general plan for the project and beyond. You should put some thought into this meeting, and treat it like any other kick-off meeting. That is to say, start how you mean to go on. Be realistic about the project and the process, but also positive. There's no good starting off all doom and gloom; you want people on your side, working enthusiastically and energetically to make the negotiation the best it can be.

This is well and truly one of those times when the quality of the inputs can have a big impact on the final outcome—so you want good quality, helpful research. Unless you're planning on doing this yourself, you'll need other people to help you. And given it's probably something they will be doing on top of their day-to-day duties, the more they understand the implications of the negotiation, and the purpose of the research, the more likely they'll be able to provide valuable input.

A couple of other key things that should happen from this meeting:

- Identify key dates.

- Agree on a meeting schedule.

- Agree what initial research will need to be done (this can always be supplemented in later meetings, but it's important to have a list that is as robust and accurate as possible at the beginning).

- Agree who will do what research.

- Agree on any communications that need to go out to the wider organisation or individuals and who these should come from.

- Develop the stakeholder analysis and communications plan and start the communications now. Be mindful of the audience and tailor the complexity of the message and the forum accordingly but keep to a consistent and regular theme. Even if nothing is happening, keep up the communication!

Agreeing the Team Roles

There will be different roles for each team member both pre, during and post negotiations. Be clear on what you expect from each person on the team, both in terms of what he or she will do and how they will do it. Make sure that each person understands how his or her part contributes to the successful negotiation.

Ensure you carefully engage both the technical skills and the personal strengths (e.g. perseverance, empathy etc.) of each individual.

Negotiation Team Behaviours

Further expanding on team roles, it is crucial to discuss and agree the team approach and behaviours. A negotiation should be approached in an organised and professional manner, so agree in advance how you are going to act and react in different situations. For example:

If things get off-track or heated (we discuss the meetings in greater detail in Chapters 7 and 8), talk about taking 'time outs' and breaks to allow everyone to calm down.

Stay professional at all times. Avoid raised voices, offensive language and never 'get personal' or take things personally. If historical interactions have meant that a particular relationship is broken beyond repair, consider if that person is the right person to be on the team.

Leave your ego at the door. A negotiation is about reaching agreement—it's not about being adversarial or aggressive. It's not about showing how clever you are. It's not about power moves and putting people in their place. Model the sort of behaviour you expect to see from the other parties. And if you behave badly, then don't get upset if the other party does too.

If specific discussions become stalled, seek agreement to move onto the next item. This will encourage the meeting to progress.

You will also find it useful to agree on discrete signals between team members should a team member get off track or perhaps start to say something they shouldn't.

Show a united front at all times. Do not disagree, undermine, argue or show discord with your team members in front of the other parties—again, call a time out if required (e.g. "can we take a few minutes, our team should discuss that further").

Debrief after all meetings. Talk about what did and didn't go well. Assign any tasks (e.g. further research, drafting of clauses) and discuss the strategy for the next session.

Case Study – Lessons Learned

A complex negotiation became very heated with a manager and a union official ending up in a stand up, yelling match across the meeting room. Eventually an official from a different union and another (external) representative of the organisation were able to stop proceedings by repeatedly insisting a break was taken.

Although the attending employees agreed that the first union official may have 'baited' the manager, they were clearly dismayed and shocked to see the manager react in such a manner and surprised that the more senior manager did not act as the organisation's lead and intervene. They also stated that it made the negotiation feel far more aggressive and personal and they were worried about the ongoing implications of their participation as employee representatives.

As a result, both managers were replaced within the organisation's team.

Key Points to Consider:

- The negotiation should be seen as a priority by management, with team selection and appropriate levels of resourcing reflecting this.

- The team should be supported by being provided with training and information on the current enterprise agreement process and environment.

- It is important to help influence the tone of negotiations by establishing positive behaviours within the organisation's negotiating team.

- Communication is critical—within the team, to the leadership team and the broader organisation and stakeholders.

Checklist – Preparing the Organisation's Negotiation Team

☑   Determine the skills, knowledge and expertise required for the team.

☑   Assign team responsibilities and roles.

☑   Identify and address any skill (etc.) gaps in the team.

☑   Ensure team members have their manager's support and are provided adequate time for enterprise negotiation activities.

☑   Provide IR information and training (as appropriate) to the negotiating team.

☑   Discuss and agree team behaviours.

☑   Develop a communication and stakeholder plan now and start communicating now!!

CHAPTER 2
Research, Research, Research

From the first few chapters, you can already see a theme emerging around how to set up the negotiation for success.

Key points to date include:

- Thinking of a negotiation as initially a project and then as an on-going process that you implement, rather than a one-off activity.

- Secondly, making sure you have the right people on the team from the start. Remember the team includes more than just the negotiators; you will also need to identify people who can help with the research and analysis (e.g. a payroll team member).

Whilst it may seem like early days, this next step is one of the most critical; and that is doing your research thoroughly and properly. So, what sort of things should you be researching and why? It's useful to break this up into three categories:

- Internal/organisational research;

- The bargaining environment research; and

- State of the nation research.

Internal Research

Internal research is about looking back to review the current document(s) for what's good and not so good. It's also about looking forward to make sure you understand what's coming in the future that will affect the negotiation.

REVIEW THE CURRENT DOCUMENT(S)

- Review any current documents, including all relevant agreements, award(s) etc. Ask around the organisation. What's good about it? What doesn't work? Are there any errors or issues? Make sure to include poor formatting, incorrect referencing and any typos!

- Make sure you speak to payroll and HR, but most importantly, talk to the line managers who use the agreement on a regular basis. Are there any clauses that really cause operational pain? What works? And what doesn't?

- A well-written enterprise agreement can be an incredibly useful document. Remember that the people who use and interpret the agreement are usually not the ones that write the document. It is critical to make sure the document is well written, in plain English and reflects what was agreed. There are plenty of agreements around where this is not the case. A poorly worded agreement can at best create confusion and at worst cause industrial conflict and disputation. You'd also be surprised how many annoying errors get rolled over agreement after agreement because people just stop properly reading the document, and just see what they think is meant to be there instead of what is actually written.

Handy Hint !

Set up a shared document that appropriate team members can access on an on-going basis so that issues can be recorded with existing agreements or awards as they are seen.

UNDERSTAND THE ORGANISATION AND PEOPLE STRATEGIES

There's no point negotiating an agreement that doesn't meet the needs of the organisation. Knowing what's coming will help you map out what should go in, what's out and what needs to change in the next agreement after this one. Is there anything coming in the pipeline that will need flexibility from the agreement, either now or in the future?

A good executive sponsor can be a great resource and pay off in this process (see Chapter 4 for more information on executive sponsors). They should be able to point you in the right direction of who to speak to, whether that's the leadership team or the Board, or some specific business unit leaders. Of course they may not be able to tell you for confidentiality or commercial reasons, but you never know unless you ask the question!

Handy Hint !

If there's a strategic planning session coming up for the operations team or relevant business area, see if you can get the upcoming negotiation on as an agenda item.

The Bargaining Environment

Research around the bargaining environment is all about the industrial relations environment both within your organisation and more broadly.

LISTEN TO YOUR EMPLOYEES!

- What's going to be on the bargaining agenda, either to be included, removed or changed and why? Is it for a broader union agenda or something specific to the organisation?

- Talk to employee delegates if you have a good relationship. Also canvass line managers and key influencers. Often items that are important or contentious to a union or employees are talked about for some time in advance. Knowing what might be on the agenda helps you research and prepare.

GET TO KNOW THE UNION(S) AND THEIR CLAIMS

- What claims have the relevant union(s) being making in other negotiations?

- Speak to your peers in other relevant companies or touch base with the industry groups or associations in your state.

- A quick search of the Fair Work Commission website will also show you agreements that have been registered. Unions and employee representatives often cite comparative examples (e.g. from competitor organisations). Knowing about those examples (whether they help your cause or not) in advance helps you to be prepared and come up with an appropriate response.

- What sort of increases and other clauses are your competitors and relevant 'like' companies and industries agreeing to?

- Get accurate wages data by:

  - Touching base with your local employer organisation if you are a member, or doing a web search for any free data that they've published.

  - Reviewing the enterprise bargaining trends data.

  - Reviewing the most up-to-date CPI data from the ABS.

- Keep a record of examples of other agreements that have been approved and are best practice or provide great examples of clauses that you can refer to.

State of the Nation Research

Take time to investigate and explore:

- What is the IR environment like at present? Is there anything happening that will influence the negotiation of this agreement (internally and externally)?

- Talk to your local industry association, employment lawyer or consultant.

- What's the political environment at the moment?

- What's your organisational workplace relations strategy? How does this negotiation fit into that? Speak to HR or the relevant business unit senior manager.

- Where does the power lie? That is, within the employee group, the delegates and the union itself.

Case Study – Lessons Learned

The political environment can have a huge impact on the local industrial environment. Many organisations found that despite very good local relationships, when the 'Work Choices' legislation was introduced, distrust became a part of negotiations at that time because of the wider political agenda of all parties.

Key Points to Consider:

- Understand your industrial relations or workplace relations strategy and how it will impact the negotiation.

- Understand the broader industrial environment and how this impacts you and your organisation.

Checklist – Research, Research, Research

☑ Plan and allocate what research needs to take place and by when.

☑ If possible, access a copy of the organisation's strategy.

☑ Review the existing document, specifically looking for issues and errors.

☑ Talk to employees about what they would like to see changed in the agreement.

☑ Do some research on the other parties to the negotiation (e.g. the union(s) and their representatives).

☑ Read up and talk to experts about the current IR environment and any trends in agreement negotiations.

CHAPTER 3

Planning Your Approach

So what and how are you going to negotiate? Now is the time to get your team together and based on your research start to prepare the organisation's log of claims 'wish list', determine the response to employees' log of claims items (if available) and work out your tactical approach. A log of claims summarises the demands from each party.

This is where having a good sense of the organisational culture and climate is important. If there is little engagement with employees, then this will set a different tone to an organisation where there is strong engagement.

Negotiation Approach

There are many approaches to negotiating, but generally most boil down to seeking either 'Win-Win' or 'Win-Lose' outcomes. That is, do you aim to seek an agreement that provides the best (in as many as possible) outcomes for all parties, or is the approach directed at 'winning' each item, and 'dominating' the other parties? Keep in mind that this may actually vary between claim items.

This is an important decision for the organisation's representatives to make consciously, as it will determine the nature and manner of the negotiation discussions.

In Chapter 1, we talked about team behaviours. When we talk about 'Negotiation Approach' what we are really talking about is how the negotiation team will represent the organisation and its actual (or aspirational!) culture and values. In fact, if your organisation has an agreed set of values, this should be your first guide. Remember, first and foremost, the agreement is between the organisation and its people.

If you don't have defined organisational values, then it is well worth agreeing some key values for the negotiation. Think about:

- Collaboration

- Professionalism

- Innovation

Of course, there is no guarantee that the other parties will follow your lead. They may well have a defined approach of their own and this can vary significantly from union to union, and even between union officials. However, your approach can influence that taken by other parties and it can influence the spirit in which an agreement is negotiated.

It is important here to note that even in a 'Win-Win' style of negotiation, at times if no workable compromise or middle ground can be found there will still be a requirement to hold a firm line on particular issues or claims. However, when negotiations get tough or heated, it's a good time to remind yourself and the negotiating team of the organisation's values. Abandoning the organisation's values when 'the going gets tough', is not a good example or precedent to set!

It's also useful to think about how you will reach agreement in principle. For example, is the principle 'nothing is agreed until everything is agreed', or will you agree each clause incrementally. The latter is certainly the more pragmatic and economical approach and if stated up front as a negotiating principle can be a very useful way to break a deadlock. However, if you agree each clause incrementally, you may find it difficult to go back and revisit a clause in the light of negotiating a different clause. This flexibility is important.

RELATIONSHIP WITH UNIONS AND DELEGATES

There is no doubt that a good relationship with unions and their delegates helps to facilitate a successful negotiation. However, if the relationship is either neutral or poor that does not mean you can't successfully negotiate. This just means there is potentially less 'behind-the-scenes tactics' available to you.

Whatever the current relationship is, look upon the negotiation as an opportunity to improve on it by displaying integrity and maintaining impeccable behaviours even in the face of poor behaviours.

CREATING THE NEGOTIATION PLAN

This is a physical (or virtual) document that details what and how you will be negotiating. At this stage it will be based on your research of what the organisation 'wants and needs' and what you believe will be demanded by the employees and/or their representatives. Keep in mind that if you are negotiating with more than one union, they will have different claims and priorities (and they may not always agree with each other), so ensure you consider all parties to the negotiation.

Once you have the actual log of claims from your employee's representatives, then you can update and maintain the plan accordingly.

It is also key that you ensure the draft has the appropriate support and endorsement (see Chapter 4) before you finalise the plan.

There are many useful planning templates available to help you through this process (an example has been included below), but as a minimum the plan should include:

- The known/expected claim items from your employees.

- The organisation's, agreed and approved, claim items.

- Your opening and final (walk away) position for each item.

- How desirable and/or crucial each item is to both the organisation and the employees.

- The potential risks/implications if each claim item cannot be agreed.

- The concessions or trades (if any) you may make for each claim item.

- The 'easy' giveaways.

- The tactics/strategies/alternative positions that you will use to achieve the desired outcome.

- The cumulative impact of any agreed claim (i.e. not just this year, but during the life of the agreement and going forward).

- The questions you will need to ask the employee representatives.

- The points to be made or relevant information provided to the employee representatives.

- What 'success' looks like.

Handy Hint ⓘ

Clearly this is a very sensitive document, so confidential document control is vital. Don't leave it on desks, printers or unattended in the negotiating room!

Negotiation Planner for Company X Enterprise Agreement
Key Objective(s): Improve flexibility and sustainability. Control rising labour costs.

Item Number	Issue/Claim Item	Company Importance/Value		Bargaining Positions Company		Opposition Expected	Opposition Importance/Value	Trades/ Concessions	Tactics
1	Wage Increase %	High	Opening	2%	Walk Away	2.5%	High	If they agree to change redundancy provisions	3% is higher than CPI
	Origin: All Parties		Ideal	2.5%	Realistic	3.0%		If they agree to remove/reduce payout of personal leave	3% is higher than area AVG
			Realistic	3.0%	Ideal	3.5%			3% equal to peer organisations
			Walk Away	3.5%	Opening	6.0%			Negotiate as final item
									Company needs to stay competitive and viable
									Start Low if they start high
									Move Up Very slowly
	Questions to Raise:								
	1. What is current CPI? - 2.5%								
	2. What are other employers paying in the area? - 2.6%								
	3. What have peer Companies agreed to ? - 3%								
2	Payout of Excess Annual Leave	Good to Have	Opening	Excess over 4 weeks	Walk Away	Excess over 4 weeks	High	Excess only > 8 weeks	Encourage employees to push unions for this to be accepted
	Origin: Company							Must be Employee's Request	Unions don't like this on principle
			Ideal	Excess over 4 weeks	Realistic	Excess over 8 weeks, Employee Requests only, One time only		Could be once off	Demonstrate that company wants people to take leave also
								Require employee to take leave equal to payout	
			Realistic	Excess over 8 weeks, employee to take = Leave	Ideal	No Change			Make their members happy
			Walk Away	Union will not Agree	Opening	No Change			
	Questions to Raise:								
	1. Are they aware that employees are asking for this?								
	2. What concerns them about this principle?								
	3. Are they aware that majority of competitor companies offer this?								
	4. What could we include in a clause to make the unions comfortable ?								

Example: Negotiation Planner Template (Microsoft Excel)

Case Study – Lessons Learned

A small manufacturing organisation commenced agreement discussions with their employees and their union representative, without being aware that the organisation could actually provide its own log of claims and negotiate its own desired changes to the agreement. The organisation had negotiated its last two agreements based only on the demands of the employees.

As a result the agreement was very dated in comparison to those of its competitors and contained clauses that severely restricted the organisation's development and profitability.

With the new negotiations the organisation's leadership was able to introduce clauses that both benefited the employees and greatly improved the longer term sustainability and viability of the organisation

Key Points to Consider:

- The negotiation approach should not be in conflict with the organisation's values.

- Ensure the negotiation approach is a positive reflection of the organisation's culture.

- Being collaborative does not mean conceding all items!

- Do you know what your organisation wants and needs from this agreement?

- You may need to review your plan and approach after meeting with the leadership team.

- Constantly review and update the plan throughout the negotiations.

Check List – Planning Your Approach

☑   Agree the negotiation approach.

☑   Establish the expected approach of the other parties.

☑   Finalise the organisation's claim items (pending approval).

☑   Develop the Negotiation Plan.

☑   Agree the specifics of each team member's role, pre, during and post the negotiations.

CHAPTER 4

Preparing the Organisation's Leaders

The reality of an enterprise agreement negotiation is that all parties to the negotiation are 'in the room' as a representative of others. This could be a union official acting on behalf of the union and its members, an employee acting on behalf of their colleagues or a manager negotiating for the organisation. Given this, as an organisation's negotiator, it is vital that you have the authorisation and support of your Executive or Leadership Team (LT). It is also important to ensure that you keep the appropriate people updated on any progress and issues, and that you know who to refer to should a matter require escalation.

Having this endorsement and communication channel will ensure that you have clear parameters under which to operate and that all appropriate parties are aware of and can quickly address any situations that may arise.

In this chapter we have assumed the involvement of an organisation's LT, however the principles and steps can be equally applied when this structure is not applicable and the decision maker is one individual, e.g. a CEO or Managing Director in a smaller organisation.

Getting the Leadership Team On Board

First, start with identifying a senior executive sponsor. Preferably this should be a member of the LT. Depending on the size and nature of the organisation, this may be an HR or Operations Director or the Managing Director. This person should be your first port of call with regular updates and issues, as well as your conduit to the broader LT.

The next step is to introduce your LT to the enterprise agreement, negotiation process and your proposed claim items. The most effective and efficient way of doing this is to provide a short presentation to the full group. Requesting a spot at one of their regular meetings is a great option.

Before presenting think about:

- Who is the best person (or people) to present to the LT? Ideally you are looking for people with internal credibility, influence and the appropriate knowledge to be able to confidently present and answer questions.

- What is the purpose of the meeting? For example, if this process is new to the LT, you may be providing context to the industrial environment and process as well as seeking endorsement more specifically.

- If they are experienced, then it may simply be to gain an understanding and endorsement around this agreement's process. Specifically:

- Endorsement of the negotiation process, approach and strategy;

- Solid agreement and approval of the organisation's claim items and their parameters;

- A comprehensive understanding of the organisation's appetite for and ability to manage any potential risks; and

- An informed, engaged and supportive LT.

It is crucial that when you enter the negotiation room, that you know what your goals, limits and level of authorities are and what the business cost of each claim item is. We will discuss the actual negotiations in Chapters 7 and 8, however, it is this stage of gaining endorsement that will help set the foundations for that negotiation. While limits sometimes have to be revisited, particularly if a negotiation gets gridlocked, it is vital that these limits are determined and locked in as tightly as possible, prior to the start of negotiations.

Presenting to the Leadership Team

Most likely you will find there are varying levels of experience and understanding within the group, so keep your presentation simple and succinct. Allow for questions (make sure you do your homework) and make the offer to provide individual briefings to any of the LT that would like further information.

Six key slides should be sufficient. Remember, keep it simple—you want to promote engaged and active discussion.

HOW DOES THE PROCESS WORK?

Provide information on the about, who, when, and how. It is also the ideal time to discuss legally required steps, inclusions and constrictions (e.g. underlying Awards, compliance tests etc.). It's a good idea to be clear on how long the process can take, as agreements can take anywhere from a few weeks through to a year to negotiate. Understanding your environment will give you the best possible chance to predict how long it will take (and don't forget to add on the process for having the Agreement registered).

THE CURRENT INDUSTRIAL ENVIRONMENT

Provide information about the external influences on the negotiation process. For example, what is happening with other agreements in your industry? What is the average agreement wage increases in your industry/location(s)? How does your current agreement compare in the marketplace? Have there been industrial disputes within your industry and/or instigated by any of the negotiating parties?

THE ORGANISATION'S CLAIM ITEMS

In Chapter 3, we discussed the process of establishing what the organisation wants/requires of the agreement and the corresponding Log of Claim items. Ensure the LT understand and endorse the key claims and help to prioritise them. Wherever possible ensure you include any cost or savings modelling of claim items. The LT may also be able to provide you with key information that may impact on these claims (e.g. key customer activity, product/service changes, strategic initiatives etc.).

THE EMPLOYEES' CLAIM ITEMS

If they have not been provided, you should indicate those that are expected, as a result of employee feedback, or current industry/union trends. Make sure you provide an update with actual claim items ASAP. Again you should provide cost or savings information, be recommending an approach and response to the claims, and seeking endorsement from the LT.

RISKS AND CONTINGENCY PLANNING

At this step it is important to discuss the internal environment, the organisation's risk management capacity and 'worst case scenarios'. Unfortunately negotiations do not always run smoothly. Explain the more common forms of industrial action, the potential implications for your organisation and what the organisation's response would/could be. Having these frank discussions in advance can significantly reduce the sense of anxiety and 'knee-jerk' reactions that can result should industrial action be threatened or actually occur.

WHAT SUCCESS LOOKS LIKE

At the end of this discussion, it is important that the LT has a good idea of what a successful negotiation looks like.

When closing, ensure you have gained endorsement for your strategy and have agreed on a process for regular updates to both the LT and all impacted employees.

Finally, it is very important to ensure these discussions and negotiation strategies are kept highly confidential. While your LT will be more than used to discussing and managing confidential information, it never hurts to provide a tactful reminder along the way. As an example, a 'confidential' watermark on the presentation slides can be very helpful.

Case Study – Lessons Learned

A manufacturing organisation's negotiations became significantly drawn out as a result of the organisation's representative's requirement to refer back to senior management for approval before agreeing to any item. In fact, the representative had not been given firm guidelines on the final wages offer and was working somewhat in the dark.

These delays created considerable frustration with all of the negotiating parties, and caused an erosion of confidence in the organisation's representative's ability and authority to reach agreement. The outcome of which, was a perception by employees that the organisation was wasting their time and not taking the negotiations seriously. This led to a very real threat of industrial action from the employee representatives.

While the situation was ultimately resolved (fortunately without industrial action), this was primarily the result of the above steps being applied rapidly, in retrospect, only when the crisis arose. It is highly likely that this crisis would not have occurred had the LT been engaged and their endorsement provided in advance enabling the representatives to negotiate with confidence.

Key Points to Consider:

- It is important to ensure that what you are negotiating has been understood and approved at the appropriate levels.

- Ensure that your team and the LT understand the financial and operational cost/implication of each claim item.

- Work on a principle of 'no surprises'. Keep your LT informed and up to date.

- You may need to circle back and review your plan and approach following your discussions with the LT.

Checklist – Preparing the Organisation's Leaders

☑   Determine and agree who will be the Executive Sponsor.

☑   Schedule a meeting with the LT.

☑   Research the industrial environment and relevant industry agreements (see Chapter 2).

☑   Prepare the LT presentation. (Anticipate and address any questions the LT may have.)

☑   Meet with the LT.

☑   Ensure LT endorsement of the claim items and negotiation strategy.

☑   With the LT, agree a regular update and issue escalation process.

☑   Follow up and report back on any outstanding issues or questions from the meeting.

CHAPTER 5

Contingency Planning

One very specific area that does need either executive or leadership team sponsorship, and some detailed planning, is the area of risk management and contingency planning.

There are three elements to this planning:

1. Assessment of the likelihood for sustained industrial action;

2. Assessment of the organisation's tolerance for risk; and

3. Developing a specific contingency plan to be implemented in the event that it all goes wrong.

What is Industrial Action?

Industrial action means when employees go on strike (i.e. refuse to attend or perform work) or impose work bans (i.e. refuse to perform all their normal duties). In response to employee industrial action, employers may lock out their employees (i.e. close the doors or gates of a workplace and refuse to allow them to work).

Under the *Fair Work Act 2009*, industrial action is defined to include the following actions:

- *Employees performing work in a manner different to how it is normally performed.*

- *Employees adopting a practice that restricts, limits or delays the performance of work.*

- *A ban, limitation or restriction by employees on performing or accepting work.*

- *A failure or refusal by employees to attend for work or perform any work.*

- *The lockout of employees from their employment by their employer.*

- *Employees and employers can only take protected industrial action when they are negotiating on a proposed enterprise agreement and that agreement is not a greenfields agreement or a multi-enterprise agreement.*

Importantly, what is key to note about industrial action is that there is the ability under the *Fair Work Act 2009* for it to be protected during enterprise agreement negotiations. That is, so long as the Act is complied with, industrial action is legal. It's important to understand this up front when developing a contingency and risk management plan.

Likelihood of Industrial Action

This is where the research that you've been doing will start to come to the fore. If you've been listening to the organisation and reading the external environment, you'll be getting some clues as to the appetite for industrial action from the employees and the union's perspective. You can also look back on the industrial history of the organisation. There are some industries and organisations, where industrial action is almost part of the game and part of the process. It's important to know all this before you start.

Consider the following:

- What is the history of industrial action at the organisation? Has anything significantly changed that would alter this dynamic?

- What is the external environment politically?

- What is the current position from that particular union?

- Has there been industrial action more generally in the sector that you work?

Now, plot the likelihood of particular industrial action versus impact of that action.

	None	Low	Mod.	High	Extreme
Definite					
Likely					
Possible					
Unlikely					
Rare					

Likelihood of Industrial Action

Impact of Industrial Action

Diagram: Risk Analysis Framework

If it looks likely that industrial action is on the cards, then get specialist legal advice now! This advice will mean you can make better decisions and you are better able to brief your stakeholders.

Tolerance for Risk

This part is actually the most important. Being clear on the internal tolerance of risk from the beginning is critical, as that will dictate to an extent the way you participate in the negotiation process.

Often, at the start of the negotiation planning process, there is a lot of table banging, chest thumping and outlandish statements made around the process and the outcomes, and who'll be getting what and who won't be. But, when push comes to shove, the reality for many organisations is that there isn't the appetite or the internal resources to support anything more than minor industrial action. Even in organisations where industrial action has been par for the course in past negotiating rounds, organisations are now seeing the damage that it does to organisational culture and trust.

The reality is also that industrial action is resource hungry, not just around replacing the labour that has been withdrawn, but defending the action in tribunals, managing internal and external stakeholders, and briefing legal representatives. There are many executive teams who weigh up the loss of potential market share or stocks, and decide the risk simply isn't worth it.

Knowing this up front is priceless. Too many negotiators have gone down a path where the Executive has talked up big, only to fold at the very last moment. It doesn't do the credibility of the negotiation team any good, and creates mistrust and distrust where it is not necessary. Remember too that there may be a short-term mentality of the organisation (i.e. the cost of the loss of one day's production isn't worth the impact of the particular claim), but it's your job to help the LT understand any longer term implications or flow on effects.

Of course, there will always be situations where the circumstances have changed when it comes time to make a decision, but understanding, as far as possible what the likely tolerance for industrial action is before embarking upon discussions, helps you plot your own internal path and plan appropriately.

PROS

- You can use it as a tactic to stand your ground.

- Locking out employees remains an option as well. But remember there are potentially huge ramifications for your brand.

CONS

- Can cause massive distrust issues going forward, often doing more damage and setting up an adversarial workplace.

- Can be extremely resource intensive; not just managing the labour withdrawal but managing the process itself.

Handy Hint

Know the value of one day's production compared with the cost of any claim/s that you are stuck on. This means you can provide information to the LT to enable them to make good business decisions around industrial action.

Developing a Contingency Plan

This is one area of negotiation where having specialist legal advice is worth the investment. If there is a history of industrial action, and you believe it is likely or you intend to have a lock out, seek advice early in the piece. This will enable you to understand exactly what industrial action means for you and your organisation and you can develop a plan around it.

It's worth scheduling in some specific time to develop a contingency plan after you've taken any necessary advice. This is not something you want to do on the run in a crisis situation.

Consider addressing the following in your thinking around the plan:

- Market share—how will industrial action impact market share/sales?

- Timing—does the potential for industrial action fall over a critical period for your business? (Often this is the case, as it allows unions to create maximum impact.)

- Resourcing—how will you resource for the labour shortage, if at all. For example, how long can you continue operating without that labour? What are the implications around running the organisation during industrial action?

- Stakeholder and sponsor engagement—who do you need to communicate with, and how will you do this to keep everyone in the loop?

- Employee engagement—how will you keep those employees engaged who do not take industrial action? How will you communicate with those who do take industrial action?

- Brand strategy—what will this mean for your external brand? Do you need any assistance with managing the PR/brand issues?

- Managing suppliers/customers—who do you need to liaise with in sales/marketing to understand and plan for the potential impact on customers and clients. Is there anything you can do to mitigate this impact?

- Legal advice—who will you use for legal advice?

- How far will you go with defending industrial action and its associated tactics such as picket lines?

- What 'war room' type mechanics will you need to put in place, to be able to plan and implement tactics?

- What other contingency planning processes do you already have in place?

Case Study 1 – Lessons Learned

After a negotiation became stalled and the threat of industrial action was raised, consultation with key operational staff and management established that the plant could be run by management for a period of up to a fortnight. This knowledge gave the organisation confidence that they didn't need to be intimidated by the threat of industrial action in the short term. When this was conveyed to unions and staff it encouraged them to return to the negotiating table in a less adversarial manner. Agreement was reached shortly thereafter.

Case Study 2 – Lessons Learned

Despite rhetoric at the beginning of the process, when push came to shove and the threat of industrial action looked very real, the leadership team of an organisation decided that the risk to the organisation's brand was worth more than the impact of conceding to a higher pay rise. Agreement was reached but the action caused significant distrust between the negotiating parties given the Employer's representatives had been holding out (based on previously agreed parameters).

Knowing the risk tolerance up front would have enabled a very different negotiation and bargaining approach from the beginning.

Key Points to Consider:

- Industrial action can be protected during a bargaining period.

- It's critical to understand the likelihood of industrial action and the tolerance for this prior to commencing negotiations, as this will inform the flavour and tone of the negotiations.

- Taking the time to specify a contingency plan up front usually means that there is more clarity than when it's done on the run and when the threat of industrial action is very real.

Checklist – Contingency Planning

☑   How likely is industrial action? Use the chart to plot the likelihood.

☑   If it is likely, do you have a good industrial lawyer? Get specialist advice now.

☑   What's the tolerance for risk within the organisation?

☑   Make sure you know your numbers. What's the value of one day of production versus the cost of the claim?

☑   What conversations do you need to have with which stakeholders to determine the risk tolerance?

☑   Do you have a contingency plan? If not, start developing a plan if there is a high tolerance for risk and a high likelihood of industrial action.

☑   Go back to your communication plan. Have you consulted with those who are key stakeholders?

CHAPTER 6

The Technical Elements

Fair Work Requirements

The *Fair Work Act 2009* provides very specific steps in negotiating an enterprise agreement. The following flowchart is taken from the Fair Work Commission's 'Enterprise Agreements BenchBook' and lists the various steps necessary to have an enterprise agreement approved. The Enterprise Agreements Benchbook can be found on the Fair Work Commission's website and contains useful guidance on the technical requirements of agreement making.

Note, that even if an agreement in principle is reached between the parties, it will not be approved by the Fair Work Commission, thus giving it no legal standing, if these steps are not complied with.

It's critical that the steps are understood including any relevant timeframes and associated paperwork.

Handy Hint ❗

Many an agreement has not been approved because the correct process was not followed. Given you've already done the hard work in reaching agreement between the parties, it pays to make sure that it doesn't fail at the last hurdle simply due to not issuing the right form or complying with the right timeframe.

BARGAINING PROCESS UNDER THE *FAIR WORK ACT 2009*

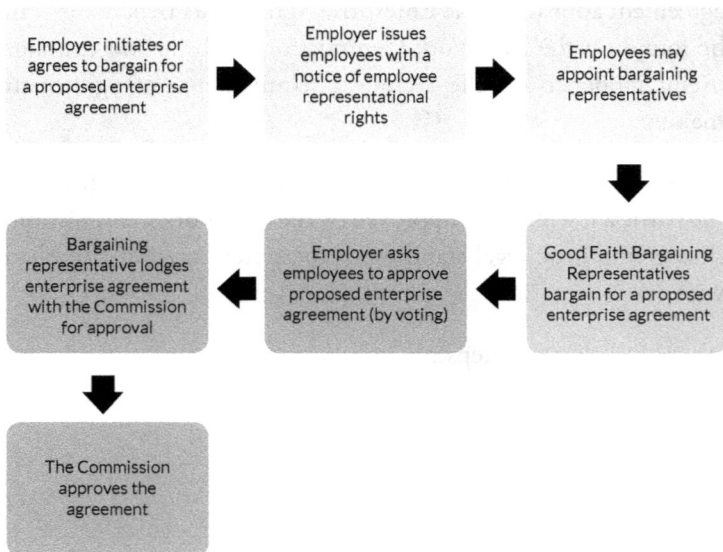

Employer initiates or agrees to bargain for a proposed enterprise agreement ➡ Employer issues employees with a notice of employee representational rights ➡ Employees may appoint bargaining representatives

⬇

Bargaining representative lodges enterprise agreement with the Commission for approval ⬅ Employer asks employees to approve proposed enterprise agreement (by voting) ⬅ Good Faith Bargaining Representatives bargain for a proposed enterprise agreement

⬇

The Commission approves the agreement

Source: Fair Work Commission – Enterprise Agreements Benchbook

Types of Agreements

An agreement can be a:

- Single enterprise agreement,

- Multi-enterprise agreement or

- Greenfields agreement (single or multiple enterprise). This is an agreement relating to a genuinely new enterprise made at a time where the employers have not yet employed any of the necessary employees.

Multi–Union Negotiations

In each of the above cases, there can also be more than one union covered by the agreement.

Many agreements cover a range of classifications and therefore the agreement may cover more than one union. This usually adds complexity to the negotiations, as each union will have its own internal agenda. At times there can also be tensions between the unions and this contributes to the complexity. Chapter 8 provides some useful tips on how to manage this.

Negotiation Parameters – Claims

There are a number of aspects of what can and can't be included in an agreement. At present, these are referred to as:

- Permitted matters

- Mandatory terms

- Unlawful content.

It is critical that prior to lodging any agreement for approval, that you check the current legislation for what's in and what's not as legislation can regularly change.

Case Study – Lessons Learned

A negotiation occurred between three unions and a single enterprise employer. There was significant tension between two of the unions. This led to a lack of clarity around the log of claims. It also led to bickering at the negotiation table, causing unnecessary conflict and angst. Ultimately, whilst agreement was reached, this was due to significant behind-the-scenes management of the relationships by the employer representatives.

Key Points to Consider:

- The *Fair Work Act 2009* has a very specific process to enable an agreement to be approved.

- An agreement can cover a single enterprise or multiple enterprises. It can cover one union or multiple unions. It can also cover a greenfields site/project.

- There is specific content that needs to be included in every agreement. There is also content that is unlawful and not permitted.

Checklist – The Technical Elements

- ☑ In your project plan, include the requirements to have an agreement approved, including specific timeframes.

- ☑ Ensure that the log of claims does not include any unlawful content.

- ☑ Ensure that you understand what type of agreement the agreement is, and comply with requirements relating to that type of agreement.

CHAPTER 7
The First Meeting

The First Meeting

We have done all of our prework and preparation. Now it is time to step in to the negotiation environment, both literally and figuratively.

The initial meeting will generally be the official handing over of the parties' claims and as a result will often include no actual negotiation. Instead its format tends to be different from the on-going meetings, as it is the first opportunity for each party to exchange and/or explain their claim items and seek clarification on the claim items of the other party.

There are a number of ways people approach the first meeting. Here we share some hints, tips and guidelines to make the first meeting an effective and positive start to interaction between the parties. Remember that the tone of a negotiation is often the sum of many smaller decisions and actions.

Prior to meeting, ensure that the right people are in the room and that the negotiating team is very clear on their particular authority for each clause. There is nothing more damaging to credibility than having to go back and check each decision 'with management'. Having said that, there will be times where it can be strategically useful to have to defer a critical decision to the most senior of the organisation (which is why they should never be part of the negotiating team). The key here is for the negotiating team to have appropriate authority and know what that authority is.

Before the Meeting

Try to make this part of the process as easy as possible with little room for conflict. That's not to say you have to provide five star catering and limousines to and from the venue; but it does make sense to have a comfortable, easily accessible venue that is convenient for all parties. It doesn't make sense to unwittingly cause conflict where there is no need.

Make sure the venue is practical with breakout rooms/areas available, free of unwanted distractions and interruptions. If possible, windows and access to fresh air (a balcony or outside area) can be useful.

Let attendees know in advance of any special arrangements relating to site access, parking etc. Also ask that they bring their diaries with them to the first meeting.

Familiarise yourself with the facilities and the nearest available phones, printers, copiers etc. You are likely to need them along the way.

For your own use, collate any reference materials that might be needed in the meeting. This would include electronic or hard copies of the existing enterprise agreement (if applicable), and any relevant award, a copy of the *Fair Work Act 2009* etc. Along the same lines, you also need to make sure that you bring along plenty of copies of any documents to be shared amongst the parties.

Start as you mean to go on!

Given the parties will often be having their first real look at the claim items, it may be a good idea to schedule a shorter session for the first meeting. This allows each team to separate and privately discuss the claim items in detail, prior to starting the formal negotiations. If this is not feasible e.g. due to people travelling large distances to attend, segment this first meeting by allowing for a significant break (e.g. lunch) following its completion.

Set the tone early. Be open, engaged and professional. Remember, it's a negotiation! There will have to be give and take and movement from all parties if agreement is to be reached. It is important to have and communicate this mindset right from the start. Don't expect other parties to be actively communicating and bargaining if your party is not. (Remember the behaviours that we covered in Chapter 1.)

The Meeting Format

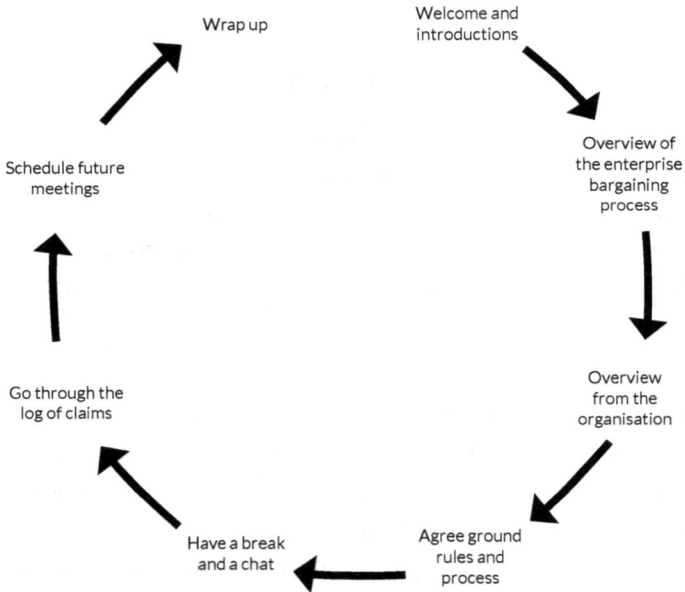

Welcome and introductions

Overview of the enterprise bargaining process

Overview from the organisation

Agree ground rules and process

Have a break and a chat

Go through the log of claims

Schedule future meetings

Wrap up

INTRODUCTIONS

As a start, take the time to go around the room and ask everyone to give a quick introduction including their name and their work area and the purpose of their attendance (e.g. employee representative, even the note-taker). If you have a large group, for the first few meetings at least, it can be well worth having name cards for all attendees.

OVERVIEW OF THE PROCESS

Take time to ensure that all parties (particularly employee representatives), have at least, a rudimentary understanding of the steps and procedures required in order to register an enterprise agreement. It is handy to have a simple PowerPoint slide prepared, just in case you need to run through the process.

OVERVIEW FROM THE ORGANISATION

Consider if it is useful to have the Managing Director or another senior representative of the organisation provide an overview of the organisation and the industry as a prelude to the negotiations. This can be helpful as it provides context to some of the discussions. BUT, it can also backfire where employee representatives view it as an attempt to 'cry poor'. It is always better to have this form of communication as part of on-going communications with employees, rather than a one off where it can be viewed cynically.

AGREE PROCESS AND GROUND RULES

'Whiteboard' and agree some process and ground rules for the negotiations. This could be everything from acceptable behaviour (e.g. letting people speak without interruption) to the start and finish times and frequency of meetings. The types of items you can agree include:

- How often will you meet? Where will you meet and what is the best duration for meetings?

- Turning off mobile phones (or putting on silent if required).

- Taking time out for teams to confer (sometimes referred to as 'caucus').

- What should happen if there is a stalemate on an item?

- Who will take the minutes and how will they be agreed?

- How will minutes and other documents be circulated?

- How will the document be drafted?

- What is the communication plan for other employees (i.e. separate, joint etc.)?

- What is the process for agreeing what is to be communicated after each meeting?

HAVE A BREAK AND A CHAT!

Schedule in a break, and if the budget allows arrange some tea, coffee and biscuits. Use the time to have some 'non-negotiation' conversations. Allow everyone to get to know each other a little and hopefully start to break down a few barriers. Try to continue this process throughout negotiations to provide 'down' time for the parties.

GO THROUGH THE LOG OF CLAIMS

Getting down to the 'nitty-gritty' . . . Asking each party to walk through each claim item may sound tedious, but claim items are often provided as a simple list and frequently the written items aren't very clear. This is the ideal opportunity for questions to be asked and clarification sought. Gaining an understanding of the issue(s) and/or reasons behind each claim item can also prove invaluable to achieving a satisfactory outcome for all parties. Many a misunderstanding has occurred because one party thought the other party wanted something that ended up being something completely different. This is particularly true where there are multiple unions involved. Make sure you understand what each claim means from every party involved and who would benefit from the claim item.

This is purely an exchange of information. Don't get defensive or start negotiating an item at this point; you are just looking for absolute clarity around what each party wants. Ask questions in a non-defensive, exploratory manner.

This is generally not the time to provide any actual response to claims, particularly if it is the first time they have been exchanged. There may be the odd exception to this (e.g. basic items like agreeing the duration of the next EBA), but in the main, it makes sense to take all claims and review them in their entirety, so you are ready to provide a considered response at the next meeting.

SCHEDULE FUTURE MEETINGS

Diaries fill up quickly and the participants may have some complex logistical arrangements to manage (e.g. different shifts, locations etc.). While you have everyone together, take the opportunity to schedule several meetings in advance. This is much easier to do in person! Also consider whether to include any social events such as a lunch or dinner to help form and build relationships. This will obviously not be appropriate in all circumstances, but there may be occasions where this assists in building the relationship between all parties.

WRAP-UP, REVIEW AND SAY THANKS

As you conclude, make sure to review any tasks assigned and include these in the minutes. Thank everyone for their time and contribution. Let them know there is an open door if anyone has any questions along the way.

EXPECTED BEHAVIOURS

In a negotiation process, there should not be any exemption from required workplace behavioural standards. Bullying, shouting, intimidation, personal insults and threats are counterproductive and have no place in an agreement negotiation, from any party. It is worth covering this in the first meeting when you work out the ground rules for the process. Remember, if things start to get heated, take a break and give everyone a chance to cool down. Most importantly, remain professional at all times. Managers can lose a great deal of respect by getting into stand up, yelling matches in a negotiation room in front of their employees.

GOOD FAITH BARGAINING

The *Fair Work Act 2009* emphasises that there is an obligation on the parties to bargain in good faith. The Fair Work Benchbook defines this as:

- "... *Good faith bargaining requirements aim to ensure that all bargaining representatives act in an appropriate and productive manner. The requirements also seek to facilitate improved communication between bargaining representatives, which is expected to reduce the likelihood of industrial action.*

- *Bargain means to discuss the terms of any transaction. Discuss means to engage in conversation, examine by argument—to debate. At its most fundamental, enterprise bargaining is about communication both before and during formal negotiations. Each requirement for good faith bargaining has as its aim, purposeful or meaningful communication.*

- *The good faith bargaining requirements do not require a bargaining representative to make concessions. A bargaining representative can meet the good faith bargaining requirements, whilst also adopting a 'hard line'.*

- *Equally, the good faith bargaining requirements do not imply moderation of demands. The good faith bargaining requirements imply a preparedness to genuinely consider offers and proposals made by other bargaining representatives and to take account of the bargaining representatives' reasons for their proposals. If, having done these things, a bargaining party is unmoved, it may still be bargaining in good faith. . "*

Case Study – Lessons Learned

One organisation chose a hard-to-reach venue with no public transport links and extremely high parking costs. There was no advice of any of this pre-meeting to the delegates. Most of the first meeting was taken up with the union furiously discussing this and how it was consistent with what they have come to expect from the organisation etc. Whilst much of this was rhetoric for the purposes of grandstanding in front of members; it was an argument that didn't need to happen. It meant that the employer was behind the eight ball from the start.

Key Points to Consider:

- A convenient, comfortable and practical venue will make for far more productive meetings.

- Advance scheduling of meetings will minimise no-shows by enabling everyone to plan and arrange their work around the meetings.

- Be clear on the expected behaviours of all parties at the beginning of the negotiation.

- 'Good faith bargaining' has a very specific definition—understanding what this means up front can assist with the general tone of the negotiation.

Checklist - The First Meeting

Before the meeting

☑ Arrange a suitable venue

☑ Advise attendees of time, venue etc. and any special arrangements (parking etc.) and to bring their diaries

☑ Collate your reference materials (enterprise agreements, awards etc.)

☑ Prepare sufficient copies of all documents to be shared at the meeting

At the meeting

☑ Introduce all parties

☑ Ensure everyone is familiar with the enterprise agreements process

☑ Agree negotiation ground rules and meeting process

☑ Agree expected behaviours

☑ Review each party's Claim items—seek clarification as required

☑ Set dates for future meetings

☑ Review and confirm action items

CHAPTER 8

The Ongoing Negotiations

With the first meeting complete, you should now have a better understanding of the other parties' claim items. You may also have a feel for their responses to the organisation's claims. However, it is generally only in the following meetings that you will get down to the real detail and actual negotiation. So it is important to prepare well for these meetings.

Be Organised

Ensure that you determine your updated response to each claim item prior to each meeting (and have gained approval as required). Keep all drafts, copies of other relevant enterprise agreements, minutes, emails and handwritten notes in an organised manner. It is very likely you will need to refer back to documents constantly throughout the negotiations and the negotiator of the next enterprise agreement will thank you many times over. Knowing why and how decisions were reached can prove invaluable if any disputes arise and during future negotiations. With turnover and career moves, there is a fairly good chance that the people negotiating this enterprise agreement will not be negotiating the next, so don't lose the history.

Handy Hint ❗

Keeping an old fashioned ring binder with all relevant information in chronological order works well and can be a good record for the organisation.

Item	Item Detail	Agreed in principle.	Disagreed and Ongoing	Claim withdrawn	Current Status/Comments
Employer & Union log of Claim items					
E1	That the current Agreement forms the basis of the new Agreement (i.e. current terms & conditions of employment continue subject to this log of claims and any relevant legislation).	X			
E2	That the new Agreement operates for a period of 3 years from 1st July 2018.	X			
E4	Classifications to be restructured.		X		Company have reviewed levels and agreed to some changes only
E3	That casual employees convert to FT after 3 months.	X			Maintained at 6 months
E5	The new Agreement preferences direct employment.	X			New wording to be finalised

Example: Meeting Log

Be Creative

Don't get fixed on one means to an outcome. Focus on the desired outcome, and then explore different avenues to reach that outcome. Test different scenarios and be prepared to take small steps forward, they are better than no progress at all.

Small steps . . .

Understand the Why

If the other party is demanding what may appear on face value to be an unreasonable request or one the organisation simply cannot meet, take the time to clearly understand the specific issue or circumstance that has led to that request. It may very well be that the issue can be managed in a different way that is satisfactory to all parties.

If you include it, you may never remove it!

What may seem like a negotiation giveaway or harmless inclusion to an enterprise agreement, it may well bite the organisation on the proverbial behind in the future. What may not impact an organisation today, may well tomorrow. So be very careful to fully understand all the implications of a clause, and why the other party wants its inclusion, before giving agreement. Never feel compelled to agree on the spot without doing the research. If you think adding something new into an agreement is hard, try taking something out.

The Numbers

Be clear on how numbers are arrived at, with spreadsheets that can be easily understood. But avoid doing too much analytics at the table, as you can easily go down a rabbit hole. Equally, there may be some people at the table who are not familiar with the numbers and who find the process disengaging and difficult to understand. If you need to build up a figure to arrive at an annualised salary rate or other, consider either taking it away and bringing it back as a proposal at the next meeting, or agreeing on a small group of people to break out, do the work separately and report back.

Developing the Draft Document

The importance and complexity of drafting clauses and the overall document is not to be underestimated. Generally this is an activity we would suggest the organisation manages. This is one key area where experienced help should be sought, as poor wording can completely change the application of a clause. This is not something that should delay progress, nor is it recommended that drafting is left until the end of negotiations. One method is to determine the main content and flavour of a clause during the meeting. The actual clause can then be later drafted to be presented and finalised at the next meeting. Where possible, some document edits can to done 'live' at the meeting. (Note: ensure all changes are clearly marked in any drafts.)

Handy Hint ❗

There is generally a recognised order when drafting an agreement. If you have limited experience with drafting or interpreting an enterprise agreement, it is worth reviewing some best practice examples of agreements to understand the general order before commencing drafting.

Negotiation Fatigue and Resilience

There comes a time in many agreement negotiations when it appears that an impasse has been reached, the negotiations may get very tense and often it will feel like no real progress is made over a number of meetings. Take heart! This is normal! Negotiating can be draining on all parties and engagement and tolerance levels can ebb and flow particularly as the more challenging and contentious items are being discussed.

This is where true negotiating skills will be tested and the ability to search for creative and mutually satisfactory options can prove invaluable. Remember, whenever possible, keep talking and exploring options. Ask the question, "what can we do to progress this?" If you are saying no to a claim, provide greater evidence and information to explain the reason behind the "no".

Using Caucuses

As explained in Chapter 7, a caucus describes a meeting break taken so that the parties can separate and privately confer amongst themselves. A caucus is particularly useful when:

- A team needs to discuss a proposal or offer;

- A team needs to discuss its response to an item or issue;

- The meeting is getting tense or heated;

- A team member has said, or is about to say something incorrect or inappropriate; or

- An additional break is needed.

Whenever possible, provide an indication of how much time is required and when the meeting will reconvene. Retire to a suitable, private location and ensure that you take all of your documents and materials with you. DO NOT leave confidential information unattended. Use caucuses as often as you need to.

Multi-union Negotiations

As discussed earlier, multi-union negotiations can add complexity to a negotiation. This is usually because of either competing/conflicting agendas or conflict between the unions at either an organisational or union level.

Being able to read the room and understand the dynamics between multiple unions is critical to successfully negotiating in this environment.

Some tips to manage multiple unions:

- Get absolute clarity on the log of claims up front and what that means for each union.

- Identify where the conflict is coming from. Is it the local representatives, and if so, what has caused this? Is there a broader ideological issue?

- Agree where particular clauses are only relevant to one union and then have break out discussions on those clauses, so as not to bog down the overall discussion. And be sure to report back so as not to be seen to be favouring one union over another.

- If necessary, consider whether to have an off the record chat with the key representatives from one or all unions to see if there's a way to move forward and still meet their needs. Or whether it is necessary to escalate to a more senior union official. This is where having good relationships can be a real bonus.

Off the Record Discussions

These are confidential, 'without prejudice' discussions between one or more individuals from the opposing negotiation teams. They can be particularly useful for gaining additional insight when an impasse is reached, as the parties may exchange sensitive information that they are not able to raise in the broader negotiation meetings.

This type of discussion is something that some employee and employer representatives will do and some will not. This is often where an IR Consultant may be able to assist. Although these conversations can be very useful, particularly when negotiations are deadlocked, if you do decide to go down this path, tread very carefully. Nothing is ever truly off the record and you are relying on the other party's discretion and integrity, as they are yours.

Before you start, be VERY specific and ensure you have all participants' agreement that the conversation is 'off the record'. This may be the time to share information and insights, but again, be very careful, particularly with confidential and/or contentious information.

And remember, be discreet, do not share the conversation with others unless absolutely necessary and in this case ensure they also understand the importance of full confidentiality.

Handy Hint !

Think about whether you would be happy with the 'off the record' conversation coming into the public record? Might there be a better way to say what you are discussing?

Grandstanding

There will be times that union representatives 'grandstand' in front of their members. Sometimes there are internal reasons for this that the company is not privy to. Sometimes it is about being able to demonstrate credibility in front of their members or the other unions. The key to dealing with this is not to get caught up in the emotion. Go back to the issue at hand, and display the behaviours you've agreed. Also try to understand what might be driving the grandstanding behaviour. Having a good relationship with union delegates at the local and the organisational level can assist with understanding what the real issue is, and how you can assist in moving it forward.

Getting Help

There can be times when an organisation will need to seek additional professional help in the form of an experienced Industrial Relations (IR) practitioner (e.g. an independent consultant or one from an industry association). This resource can bring objectivity and a different perspective into the negotiations, as well as acting as a facilitator to help manage the meetings and keep things moving. An IR practitioner will often have relationships with the key players within unions that can be useful.

An IR practitioner can also provide a greater insight into broader industry trends and benchmark agreements and clauses.

Keep Up the Two Way Communication with Staff

Waiting for updates and information can be quite frustrating for those not present in the negotiation room and let's face it, you cannot always be 100% sure that the discussions are being accurately communicated to impacted employees by the employee representatives.

Ideally, joint updates to staff (i.e. from all parties) can be quickly agreed and distributed after each meeting. Where this cannot occur, ensure the organisation provides these updates (written and/or verbal) to its impacted employees in a timely manner. Keep the updates informative, accurate and factual. No matter how difficult the negotiations are, resist the opportunity to make pot shots at the employee representatives. It just looks petty and unprofessional.

Make sure your managers and supervisors are also fully updated immediately after the meetings, so they can answer employee questions or direct them to the right people in your negotiating team. Also ask them to update your team with any employee feedback or 'scuttlebutt'. This can be vital as it is not unheard of to find that the views and priorities of the greater employee population are not being truly reflected by their representatives, who may have their own personal or organisational agendas.

Handy Hint !

Remember that even if there is seemingly no news, keep the communication open and up-to-date. No information creates a vacuum in which rumours thrive and grow.

Don't Make it Personal!

You and your team are negotiating on behalf of your organisation. The employee representatives and union officials are negotiating on behalf of their colleagues and members. Like you, they will also have their external pressures and instructions. Acknowledge and respect that.

Case Study 1—Lessons Learned

One negotiation came to a screeching halt with the company's desire to introduce a performance management system to production staff. However, the representative union did acknowledge that there was a need for development discussions and for supervisor feedback (which frequently only occurred when issues reached a warning stage). So the compromise was that once a year there would be a one-on-one, informal discussion to cover these topics.

Case Study 2—Lessons Learned

In a manufacturing plant, one union was completely against the cashing in of annual leave, even though it was highly desired by the employees. In short, the union was (quite reasonably) concerned about work/life balance and the implications of people not taking leave. As the company actually shared that concern, the meeting of the minds was a clause that provided a once off opportunity to cash in leave, which required employees to actually take leave, equal to any cashed in.

Key Points to Consider:

- Nothing is final, until the entire agreement has been successfully negotiated. Until then, even 'agreed' clauses are considered 'agreed in principle' until the entire agreement is finalised.

- Negotiation may be relatively quick, or long and drawn out. In every case it is important to keep all relevant parties informed and up-to-date.

- Stay open-minded and ask lots of questions during negotiations. Understand what is really important to your employees and why this is the case.

- Even when frustrated, it is important to maintain a professional approach with the opposing parties. It is very likely you will still be working together long after the agreement is registered.

Checklist – The On-going Negotiations

☑   Maintain complete records and files.

☑   Determine who will draft clauses on behalf of the organisation. Is a legal review required?

☑   Draft clauses throughout the course of the negotiations for review in meetings.

☑   Ensure appropriate behaviours are communicated and maintained at meetings.

☑   Fully discuss and understand the reasons behind all claims, particularly those in dispute.

☑   Get help if you need it.

☑   Ensure accurate and timely updates are provided to (and from) impacted employees.

CHAPTER 9

So It's All Over

So, you've finished the negotiations, and there is an agreement in principle. Remember that it's not finished until it is registered with the appropriate authority. Ensure you review the authority's documentation (e.g. The Fair Work Commission has an excellent website covering enterprise agreement negotiations and registration) to ensure you meet all current requirements.

Selling the Agreement

Once you have an agreement in principle, it will need to go to a vote. Here's where you may need to help sell the agreement to the rest of the employees. Remember that the ones that were in the room understand the process of how each claim was negotiated, but this won't be true for the wider employee population; so being able to join the dots for them is really important. To the extent that is possible, be as united as possible when presenting the agreement.

Remember to present the agreement in a way that explains the terms but also what those terms will mean for the employees and the impact it will have.

Registering the Agreement—Pre-approval Steps

Many employers have come unstuck by not following these steps and meeting the appropriate timelines.

EXPLAINING THE TERMS OF THE AGREEMENT

As the employer, you need to explain to your employees the terms of the agreement in a way that is appropriate given your workforce. So, for example, if you have a number of employees with English as a second language, you will need to make sure that the employees understand the terms of the agreement. You can do this by either providing a simple document that explains in plain English the terms of the agreement or by making sure there is an appropriate interpreter available.

THE VOTE

Employees must vote on whether to accept the agreement or not. This vote cannot take place until 21 days after the notice of representational rights has been issued.

Seven days prior to the vote the following needs to occur:

- Employees need to be told of the vote (when, where and how). The how refers to the method of voting, such as secret ballot run by the Electoral Commission, ballot run by the company/representative union or show of hands.

- Employees need to be given a copy of the agreement and any other material incorporated by reference (i.e. the award, the National Employment Standards etc.).

- There is a reasonableness test associated with giving every employee a copy of the documentation. One way to ensure compliance is to provide every employee with a summary document of the key terms and conditions (particularly any changes). Then ensure that copies of the full agreement are available on noticeboards, in the lunchroom, at handovers, at team briefings or shift huddles, with union representatives and with managers, supervisors and team leaders. Make sure that it is very clear where employees can access the full documents.

The agreement is successfully voted when a majority of employees of the relevant organisation cast a valid vote.

WHAT YOUR AGREEMENT NEEDS TO INCLUDE AND CANNOT INCLUDE

Prior to circulating your agreement out to vote, you'll need to double-check the following.

Firstly, does the agreement contain the following clauses?

- a coverage clause

- a nominal expiry date

- a flexibility clause and a consultation clause and

- a dispute settlement procedure.

There are model examples of all these clauses available on the Fair Work Commission's website.

Secondly, make sure the agreement does not contain any unlawful content (see Chapter 6).

All agreements also need to pass the Better Off Overall Test (BOOT). This is a critical part of the approval process, and involves ensuring that the terms and conditions you have agreed to mean that the employees who are covered are better off than if they had remained under the relevant modern award and National Employment Standards. There is a comparison of terms that needs to take place, particularly if you are fundamentally changing terms (for example, offering an annualised arrangement), that demonstrates the employee is better off under the new agreement.

What Happens if the Vote Fails?

There will be times when despite the best efforts of all involved, the vote is not successful. In this case, the key is understanding why the vote failed:

- Is the 'no' vote a political statement?

- Is there a specific term or clause that is a sticking point?

- Is it an issue with how the agreement was communicated?

- Is the issue that the unions are not supportive of the agreement and weren't selling it?

- Is there a lack of understanding?

A 'no' vote is always disappointing, particularly after the effort involved with negotiating an agreement in principle. But a no is rarely fatal. Take some time to understand the issues and then regroup with the LT and the organisation's negotiation team to review the strategy and agree the next steps.

Having your Agreement Approved

Once the agreement has been 'made'(i.e. voted by a valid majority of employees), then a bargaining representative has 14 days to apply to the Fair Work Commission for approval of the agreement.

There are specific forms that need to be completed by all parties.

The documents can be lodged via email, express post, fax, in person or electronically.

In order to approve an agreement, the Fair Work Commission will need to be satisfied on the following:

- the agreement has been made with the genuine agreement of those involved

- the agreement passes the better off overall test

- the agreement does not include any unlawful terms or designated outworker terms

- the group of employees covered by the agreement was fairly chosen

- the agreement specifies a date as its nominal expiry date (not more than four years after the date of Commission approval)

- the agreement provides a dispute settlement procedure and

- the agreement includes a flexibility clause and a consultation clause.

TIMELINE DEPENDENCIES

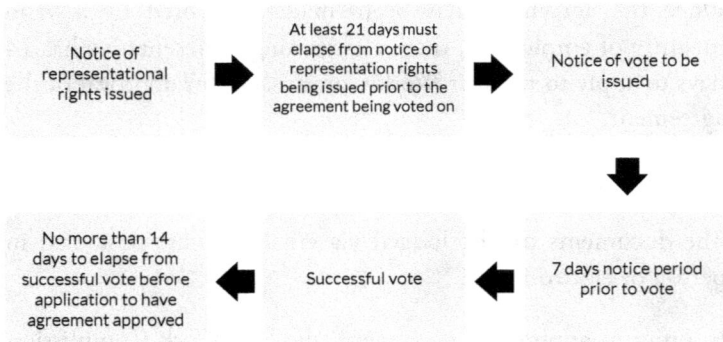

Post Agreement

An enterprise agreement negotiation is not a one-off process that culminates in the successful approval of the document. It is usually an on-going process, whereby the successful approval resets the process once again.

There are three steps to the post agreement phase:

WRAP UP OF CURRENT NEGOTIATION:

- If at all possible, it is recommended that a meeting takes place with key delegates and other key operational personnel where each clause is read through and joint understanding/ agreement reached on the interpretation.

- Meet with payroll to go through the agreement in detail, particularly any changes to terms and conditions.

- If relationships permit, a joint debrief and review of the negotiation with all parties can be very useful. What worked well and what didn't? What can be learnt? In a very bitter or difficult negotiation, this is not always possible of course. If it's not possible, at the very least ensure this review takes place with the organisation's representatives and that someone takes responsibility for documenting this project review and debrief. Three years between agreements is a long time; memories fade and people move on.

- If relationships permit, a celebration of some kind is often a nice way to end the process. Even a simple morning tea or lunch can be a good way to celebrate. If relationships are strained, make sure that the organisation's negotiation team get a thank you and some form of recognition for what is often a hard slog with little recognition or reward!

Implementation

Implementation is key! Too often, hard won clauses are incorrectly implemented or forgotten completely.

- Communicate, communicate, communicate. Make sure that the terms and conditions are simply explained (including why they were introduced) to the wider employee group.

- Ensure that relevant clauses are identified and implemented correctly.

- Timeline any future clauses that need to be implemented at a later point in the agreement.

Prepare for the Next Agreement

Make life easier for yourself when negotiating the next agreement by preparing well in advance.

Report progress on any activities agreed to in the agreement.

Keep a log of all EBA related issues (e.g. ambiguities, restrictions to operations etc.).

Make sure that communication is open and frank during the agreement, including any commentary on the state of the business.

Start the cycle again **well in advance** of the nominal expiry date of this agreement.

Case Study – Lessons Learned

An organisation wanted to radically change terms and conditions because of their financial state. They started the communication about the finances of the business well in advance of the expiry of the current agreement, and made sure to include employee representatives. The discussions were frank and open. When it came time to renegotiate the agreement, trust had been created.

Contrast this with many examples of where organisations stand up and give a dire 'state of the nation' address just before commencing negotiations. Employee representatives are often cynical of the motive (and accuracy) of such statements and it often means the negotiations don't get off to a good start.

Key Points to Consider:

- Consider the communications approach to 'selling' the agreement.

- Make sure all the steps are complied with in terms of the requirements of the Act.

- Once the agreement is approved, it is necessary to have a review and implementation process.

- Enterprise bargaining is not a one-off event that occurs every three years, it is an on-going process.

Checklist – So It's All Over

☑   Have you developed a strategy to sell the agreement? Is it a joint strategy?

☑   Have you created a simple document to explain the terms of the agreement in a way that meets the requirements of the Act?

☑   Have you complied with the requirements of the Act to lodge the agreement?

☑   Have you undertaken the BOOT test?

☑   Have you completed the relevant paperwork to lodge the agreement?

☑   Have you developed a review and implementation plan?

☑   Celebrate!

ADDITIONAL RESOURCES

CPI data:
abs.gov.au/ausstats/abs@.nsf/mf/6401.0

Enterprise bargaining trends data you can access via this website:
employment.gov.au/trends-federal-enterprise-bargaining

AWRS data centre:
fwc.gov.au/creating-fair-workplaces/research/australian-workplace-relations-study/awrs-data-centre

Useful information from the Fair Work Commission:
benchbooks.fwc.gov.au/enterpriseAgreements/; fwc.gov.au/awards-and-agreements/agreements/approval-process

National Employment Standards:
fairwork.gov.au/employee-entitlements/national-employment-standards

SOME THANK YOUS

The idea for this book emerged from one Linked In post that grew and grew!

It is true that any book that goes from an idea in the authors' mind to an actual printed copy is a combination of many people's guidance and contribution, and this one is no exception.

And so, we would like to express our many thanks to our families for their patience, love and ongoing support. Tammy would like to have a special call out to her husband Alex who proofs every version of every book she writes.

Thanks to our early readers, Jodie Beeson, Julie Fairweather, Michael Paynter and Helen Falls. Your suggestions and comments were invaluable and have helped to make this book the best version possible.

Thank you to Deputy President Geoff Bull and Kylie Groves for your kind and generous reviews.

Finally, many thanks to Kelly Exeter for the cover and design and to Kym Campradt for her editing and proofing.

INDEX

www.ingramcontent.com/pod-product-compliance
Lightning Source LLC
Chambersburg PA
CBHW071230290326
41931CB00037B/2563